Faure Must Go

Dwayne Wong (Omowale)

ISBN: 1720738807
ISBN-13: 978-1720738800

DEDICATION

To my brothers and sisters in Togo. A luta continua.

CONTENTS

1 INTRODUCTION

I decided to begin my efforts at building a Pan-African movement in October 2017. I launched what I called the Movement for Restoring the African Mind. The purpose of the movement that I began organizing was to restore the thinking of African people. In my view the greatest obstacle that confronts African people is our colonized way of thinking, so I felt that addressing that issue was the most critical step in liberating African people.

I also intended for the Movement for Restoring the African Mind to be part of my effort to rebuild the global Pan-African struggle. By the time I was born, in 1991, the global African struggle had been in decline all across the world. Guyana received its independence from England in 1966, the same year both of my parents were born. The Guyana that I was born in had been independent for decades. People my age never experienced colonial rule in the Caribbean or in Africa. People my age never experienced Jim Crow in the United States. In fact, people who are my age would not even remember apartheid. I remember when I first heard that Nelson Mandela was the first black president of South Africa, I was confused. How could an African country elect its first black president in the 1990s? At the time I knew nothing about apartheid or colonialism. In a sense I was born into a generation of people of African descent that were freer than our parents and grandparents, yet I also came to recognize that I was also born into a generation without a clear direction. The struggles of African people persisted, but those struggles were now being waged in a manner that was more disorganized than the struggles of previous generations.

The global struggles of African people have continued, but it continued in a mostly disconnected way. In the 1960s, for example, there were bonds between Africans in the United States that were fighting against oppression in their country and those in Africa that were fighting for independence from colonial rule. During this period you also had figures like Malcolm X who actively worked to unify those struggles. In the 2000s there was no such unity. This was largely done by design. The Pan-African movement of the 1960s had been deliberately destroyed.

The Federal Bureau of Investigation (FBI) played an instrumental role in that process of destruction so that by the 1980s there was no movement. Malcolm X and Martin Luther King had been assassinated. The Black Panthers were destroyed due to a combination of FBI persecution and internal issues within the Panthers. Many of the prominent figures among the Panthers were either killed or imprisoned. The Republic of New Afrika was under similar pressures from the FBI and it was eventually destroyed. It was the same for the Black Liberation Army. All of these individual leaders and organizations were wiped out. Not only was the movement destroyed, but our communities were destroyed as well and this had the effect of limiting the potentials of African people. The revolutionary spirit of the 1960s was broken and black communities were left awash with guns, drugs, and gang violence.

Most of the Caribbean received its independence, but the situation in the Caribbean had not radically improved with this independence. A Black Power movement emerged there in the 1960s, but it too was extinguished. Walter Rodney, one of the prominent Pan-Africanists in the Caribbean at the time, was assassinated in 1980. Not long after this Maurice Bishop was assassinated in Grenada and the revolution in Grenada died with Bishop. Makandal Daaga, who came to prominence as the leader of the 1970 Black Power movement, made several failed attempts to run for political office in Trinidad. In 2012, Daaga joined the People's Partnership coalition, which was led by the United National Congress political party. For many of Daaga's supporters joining such a coalition was seen as a betrayal of the values that Daaga once stood for.

There was a systematic attempt in the Caribbean

to suppress the Black Power movement. I have written about this often in my books. Examples of this include Walter Rodney being banned from Jamaica, Kwame Ture being barred from returning to Trinidad, and Errol Barrow's attempts to stifle freedom of speech to suppress the Black Power activists. I also came across a copy of the Saint Vincent government gazette from April 17, 1971. It lists a large number of people who were restricted from going to Saint Vincent. This was how widespread the attempt to stifle the Black Power movement was. As I wrote about in *Malcolm X, Bob Marley, and Other Essays*, even the Rastafarian movement that emerged in the Caribbean was met with repression from various Caribbean governments. There was a very hostile reaction to Black Power and any attempts to uplift the suffering Caribbean masses.

There was also an attempt to destroy the Pan-African movement in Africa. African leaders like Kwame Nkrumah, Patrice Lumumba, Sylvanus Olympio, Thomas Sankara and others who wanted real independence for Africa were all eliminated. The same forces that eliminated Africa's genuine leaders were also the forces that propped up and supported puppet regimes, like the one in Togo. Colonialism ended in Africa, but the colonial relationship still remained. This is a situation which has been described as neocolonialism. African nations were now politically independent, to a certain degree, but the foreign economic control of Africa persisted.

By the time I grew into adulthood there were

certainly many people who spoke of Pan-Africanism, but I could point to very few people who were engaged in the level of Pan-African organizing that we saw in the past. In 2014 there were protests in Ferguson in response to the killing of Mike Brown. That same year there were also protests in Haiti against the corrupt government of Michel Martelly and there were also protests in Burkina Faso that toppled the dictatorship that was in power there. I was seeing all of this going on in 2014 and I felt that we should have been making a greater effort to unify the different struggles being waged by African people. It has taken me a few years, but I am now in a position where I can assist with building that unity.

As I said, in October 2017 I set out to do my part in rebuilding the movement that was destroyed. In August of that same year the people of Togo began protesting for an end to fifty years of dictatorial rule. At the time that I began working on my movement I was aware of the situation that was taking place in Togo and I felt that it was my responsibility as a Pan-Africanist to do whatever I could to support the struggle there, especially since I had not seen too many of the Pan-Africanists in the diaspora speaking out about what was taking place in Togo. One of the goals for the movement that I was building was to form a unified front among Pan-Africanists so that we can support each other's struggles, so this also fit in with the objectives of my movement as well.

Togo is a nation that has been ruled by a single family for more than fifty years. Under the

Gnassingbé dynasty Togo has been one of the poorest and most miserable countries in the world. The people of Togo have had to endure poor living conditions, which have included lack of access to clean drinking water and abysmal healthcare—Togo is a country where women are made to give birth to their babies on hospital floors. Worst of all is the horrific brutalities that the people of Togo endure for daring to speak out against these conditions. Arbitrary arrests, torture, and outright murder have all been tactics that the regime in Togo has used to silence dissent. In one of her blog posts, Farida Nabourema gave the following accounts of women who were tortured simply for being the wives of people who were wanted by the police in Togo:

> Ms. Komlan and Ms. Yao were the wives of two gents who were arrested in the armed robbery case of a store called Marc Lei located in Tokoin Amoutievé in Lomé (capital city of Togo). Their husbands together with another man were arrested by Togolese gendarmes and were accused of being responsible for the robbery. Mr Komlan and his comrades were then brutally beaten and tortured by the gendarmes to force them to confess to the crime. But they denied it despite the torture they were subjected to.
>
> In order to obtain their confessions, the Togolese gendarmes decided to arrest the wives of these men. They went to the pregnant Mrs. Komlan's house and took her under their custody for a "forceful interrogation." The police asked Ms. Komlan to denounce her husband and

confess that he was responsible for the crime he was being charged with. But just like her husband, she denied the charges. The gendarmes therefore chose to use a wild method to obtain confessions from the lady. They undressed her, wrapped her breasts with electrical cords and electrocuted her through the breasts. The lady, who was pregnant at the time, miscarried her baby during the process. Notwithstanding, her pain, cries and even the blood that was rolling on her did not soften the heart of the gendarmes who continued to shock her till she lost consciousness.

Ms. Yao was arrested for the same reasons; the "Marc Lei" robbery case. She had just given birth to a baby and was living in a small room in a popular neighborhood of Lomé. When the police went to her house to arrest her, she was with her baby at the time of the arrest. They took her away and left the baby all alone on the bed. Despite her pleadings to find a guardian for her baby while she was being taken away, the officers refused to give in. The baby died of hunger and heat few days later and the neighbors only found out days later when his body was decomposing and the smell was becoming unbearable.

This is a regime that has been so cruel that even children have been targets of their brutality. In 2013 the government killed Anselme Sinandaré, who was an elementary school student who was protesting because the teachers were on strike and he wanted to go back to school. Given conditions such as this, it is no surprise that the people of Togo decided to rise up in protest. The protests began on August 19, 2017. This was not the first time the people of Togo rose up in protest. Much like the protests of the past, the government of Togo responded by sending their troops to brutalize and kill the protesters. What caught my attention about this situation was that the people of Togo decided to fight back. Some of the protesters captured the soldiers and beat them. Others chased away the soldiers by throwing things at them. My favorite picture from the protests was one of a woman dragging one of the soldiers to safety after he was captured and beaten by the protesters.

The initial reaction of the government to these protests was to use their usual methods of repression and violence. At one point the government even attempted to cut off the internet, but this tactic backfired. The activists in Togo were able to use their network to get information outside of Togo. The government, on the other hand, was not able to counter the information that the opposition was sending to international media outlets because of the internet shutdown. Cutting off the internet or restricting internet access has become a common tactic used by repressive African governments to stifle their population. This was done by Joseph Kabila in the Democratic Republic of Congo to stifle protests there. In Tanzania, President John Magufuli introduced regulations that would charge bloggers over $900 to publish their content, which was done as part of Magufuli's effort to stifle criticism of his government.

One issue that has confronted Africa since the end of colonial rule is that leaders refuse to give up power, which leads to situations in which these leaders often have to be forced out of power. We saw this in Zimbabwe with Robert Mugabe, whom I have previously written about in *Africa-Man: A Collection of Pan-African Writings*. Mugabe was in power in Zimbabwe from 1980 until he was deposed by the army in 2017. This has been the general trend across Africa. Zambia, which was formerly Northern Rhodesia, gained its independence in 1964. Kenneth Kaunda was the nation's first president and was their only president until 1991 when the opposition won in a landslide victory against Kaunda. For decades Kaunda ruled Zambia as a one-party state and refused to give up power, despite his woeful management of Zambia's economy in the years that he served as president. Those who opposed Kaunda were detained and treated terribly. One report noted that alleged abuses "include beatings, withholding of food, pain inflicted on various parts of the body, long periods of solitary confinement, and threats of execution."

In Mali, Modibo Keita was deposed in 1968. Moussa Traoré took over and he remained in power until he himself was deposed in 1991. Omar Bongo Ondimba became the second president of Gabon in 1967 and he remained in power until his death in 2009. Omar was replaced by his son Ali Bongo Ondimba, who continued his father's dictatorial rule. Omar was one of the richest men in the world, with his presidential palace in Libreville, Gabon's capital, costing $500 million. Hastings Banda became the president of Malawi in 1966. In 1993, due to international pressure, Banda was forced to end the one-party rule in Malawi. In 1994, Banda's party was defeated, ending his brutal rule. One example of Banda's brutality was when three cabinet ministers and a member of parliament were attempting to create reforms in the government. They were arrested and beaten to death with sledgehammers.

Cameroon became independent in 1960. From 1960 until 1982, the nation was run by Ahmadou Ahidjo. When he resigned he was replaced by Paul Biya who has been president of Cameroon ever since. In the Gambia, Dawda Jawara served as president from 1970 until he was deposed in 1994. That coup brought Yahya Jammeh into power and Jammeh would remain in power until he was defeated in the election that was held in December 2016. Jammeh did not concede defeat until January of the next year, however. The former Spanish Guinea gained its independence and became Equatorial Guinea in 1968. Francisco Macías Nguema was elected as the nation's first president and he remained in this capacity until 1979 when he was overthrown and executed by his nephew, Teodoro Obiang Nguema Mbasogo. Mbasogo has been the president of Equatorial Guinea since 1979.

In the Republic of the Congo a Catholic priest named Abbé Fulbert Youlou became the first president in 1960. He was deposed in 1963. This would be the first of many coups in the Republic of the Congo. The most recent came in 1997 when

Pascal Lissouba was deposed by Denis Sassou Nguesso. Nguesso served as the president from 1979 until 1992. Pressure from the international community forced Nguesso to hold democratic elections. He was defeated in the 1992 elections, but would return to power again during the Congo's second civil war. Nguesso has been the president of the Congo since 1997. In Angola, José Eduardo dos Santos served as president from 1979 until he resigned in 2017. In Guinea-Bissau, which, like Angola also fought a war of independence against the Portuguese colonizers, the African Party for the Independence of Guinea and Cape Verde was established as the sole party in Guinea-Bissau under the leadership of Luis Cabral, who was the half-brother of Amilcar Cabral. Cabral was overthrown in a coup in 1980 and replaced by João Bernardo Vieira. Viera served as the president of Guinea-Bissau for three terms, and during his second term he was overthrown as the result of a civil war. These are just some of the examples of dictatorial African leaders who refused to concede power. In *Kingdoms and Civilizations of Africa* I pointed out that prior to colonial rule Africa did have its own system of checks and balances which limited the powers of the ruler, as well as customs that were put in place to remove poor rulers, so this issue of incompetent and corrupt leaders who refuse to relinquish their power is part of the negative legacy that colonialism left behind when it dismantled traditional African institutions.

With the ongoing protests taking place in Togo I was determined to do whatever I could to assist that struggle. To achieve this I reached out to Farida Nabourema, an activist from Togo who has been involved in Togo's fight for liberation since she was a teenager. She is a co-founder of the Faure Must Go movement and the executive director of the Togolese Civil League. I first became aware of Farida when I saw a report about a woman who snuck into Togo and recorded footage of how terrible the infrastructure in Togo was. At the time the government of Togo had been lying to people by telling them that the infrastructure was being developed in the country, so Farida felt that it was necessary to go to Togo herself to expose the government's lies. This had upset the government so much that they sent police officers from house to house in search of Farida. They also put out stories alleging that Farida was a prostitute from America.

This was in 2016. I was really impressed by the courage of this woman. I would hear about Farida again when she was interviewed by Sahara TV regarding what was taking place in Togo. I was impressed by her answers to the questions. She spoke about how Africans did not need to run to the United States or France to take care of their problems, especially since France was responsible for the situation in Togo. She also spoke about the need for structural changes to Togo's political system, so that no one could abuse their powers in the way that the Gnassingbé family has done. After watching a few more videos with Farida, I decided to reach out to her to see what I could do to help the people of Togo in their struggle. Farida told me that the best thing that I could do to help the people of

Togo was to assist with raising awareness for their struggle, so that is what I have been working on. At the time I was a contributor at Huffington Post, so I used that platform to write articles to inform people about what was taking place in Togo.

I began by writing an open letter to Faure expressing my views on the protests in Togo from the perspective of an African in the diaspora who was distressed to see what was taking place in Togo:

> Dear President Faure Gnassingbé, I am not a citizen of Togo, but I am the descendant of people who were forcibly taken from the African continent. Many of my ancestors could have very well been taken from Togo. It is for this reason that I address you as a member of the African diaspora who is concerned about what I see taking place in my ancestral homeland. What especially troubles me about what is happening in Africa is the fact that our ancestors fought so hard to achieve their liberation, but now their sacrifices are being wasted because of greedy and selfish leadership.
>
> As a people we have endured tremendous suffering for the past five centuries. Our ancestors were forcibly taken from Africa in chains and brought to the Americas where they were enslaved. Our ancestors were forced to labor without pay, all while enduring beatings, torture, and rape. We did not passively accept that enslavement and we fought back. There were revolts against slavery throughout the

Americas. After slavery was abolished we continued to endure hardships such as colonialism in the West Indies and Jim Crow in the United States, and we continued to fight back.

Not long after slavery was abolished the scramble for Africa began. The people of Africa were violently conquered and subjugated by the colonial powers of Europe. Under colonial rule Africans endured much of the same beatings and tortures that we endured here in the Americas. One of the worst examples of the abuses that Africans endured was in Namibia where the German colonizers committed genocide against the people there. Africans did not passively accept being oppressed under colonial rule. They fought colonialism and overcame it.

I recount this history to remind you President Gnassingbé that we African people are not a passive people who accept oppression without resisting. The people of Togo have certainly demonstrated this. You have responded to the peaceful demands of the Togolese people with violent force, but the people of Togo will not be silenced. They have endured a dictatorship that has lasted fifty years and do not intend to endure this dictatorship for much longer.

President Gnassingbé you must understand that in the past more powerful men than you have tried to suppress African people and have failed. African people confronted Europe's most powerful empires, such as the British and French empires, and won our independence from them.

You may use violent force to murder and suppress the people of Togo, but that is nothing new for us. The United States and South Africa both used violent force against African people to maintain Jim Crow and apartheid. That use of violent force failed for both of them and it will fail for you as well.

During the days of slavery and colonialism we were made to believe that we were a primitive and savage people with no history. We were made to believe that it was Europeans that brought civilization to us. Those of us that have taken the time and effort to study our history know that this is not true. We know that Africans have produced great civilizations, but the pride that we have in our past accomplishments is tainted by the fact that Africa today does not truly reflect what we as African people are capable of achieving. President Gnassingbé it is leaders like yourself that are responsible for this and it is for this reason that I write this letter to inform you that your regime has not only caused terrible suffering for the people of Togo, but it is also a betrayal of the sacrifices of our ancestors because our ancestors did not fight so that men such as yourself could continue to oppress Africans as the colonial masters of the past did. But we are a resilient people, and as I pointed out, we have overcome great obstacles in the past. President Gnassingbé history will remember you as being one of those obstacles that tried, but ultimately failed to keep African people suppressed.

When I wrote *Jumbie Tales* in 2015 one of the stories in my book was about the spirit of an African who was taken away in the slave trade possessing the body of a diplomat so that he could return to African to confront and chastise one of the corrupt politicians there. For many years I have been very angered by what these so-called leaders have done to Africa, the land that my ancestors were forcibly taken from, so I wrote this letter to express these feelings directly to one of the worst of those leaders. Farida described the letter as beautiful and even offered to translate it into French so that it could be shared among the Togolese people. Many Togolese who read it on social media took it upon themselves to translate it.

The reaction I received for writing this letter from the people of Togo, and other West Africans, was very inspiring for me and was somewhat unexpected. When I began writing about Togo I did so in an attempt to inform African Americans and others in the diaspora who were not aware of what was taking place in Togo. I especially wanted more Africans in the diaspora to know about Farida, the courageous young activist who was bravely standing up for her suffering people. I felt that we in the diaspora could use more fearless activists like Farida. I was successful in my efforts to educate the diaspora on Togo, but what I did not expect was the support that I would receive from the people of Togo and others in West Africa. I quickly realized that I was not only writing articles to educate African Americans, but I was also writing to motivate the people of Togo in their struggle.

I was not born in Togo, but I found myself being welcomed by the Togolese people as a fellow African in the struggle for Togo's freedom. I have even described feeling like a Togolese myself because so many of the people of Togo recognized me as someone whose ancestors were taken from their land. One brother was so gracious enough to let me know that he had family in Togo, so that if I ever had a desire to go to Togo there was a place for me to stay. There were others who were even talking about giving me an honorary Togolese citizenship for my efforts to assist the struggle in Togo.

Writing about Togo provided me with my first real opportunity to build a meaningful type of Pan-African unity among the Africans in the diaspora and those on the motherland. As I said, at the time that I decided to launch my efforts with building a Pan-African movement the protests in Togo were ongoing and I felt that those of us in the diaspora who consider ourselves to be Pan-Africanists should do everything in our power to support the people of Togo as they fought to free themselves from five decades of neocolonial domination. One of the things that I would come to find is that there is a very strong Pan-African sentiment among the Togolese people, especially Farida.

Farida has deep family ties to the revolutionary struggle for freedom in Togo. Her grandfather, Allassani, was someone who suffered greatly for opposing French colonialism in Togo. He was arrested in 1948 for refusing to pay taxes to the French administration. He later joined the

Committee for the Unity of Togo (CUT), which was a political party that was demanding independence for Togo. Allassani began spreading the-news of the independence struggle in his village. For this he was arrested, stripped naked, and beaten by French soldiers. The hardships continued as the French decided to deny access to healthcare to those who opposed French colonialism. Farida explained that her grandmother lost many babies because of this, including Sani who was only two years old when he died due to measles. Sani's death was especially devastating for Allassani. In her blog Farida writes of her grandfather's final days:

> My grandfather's health deteriorated and he died on December 25 1999. Before passing away, he told my father that his only wish was to see the neocolonial regime of Eyadema fall so he could carry the news of their victory to our martyrs but he entrusts him with the struggle. Unfortunately, two generations later, the struggle continues and I hope my children will not inherit it. I have been accused of having a personal vendetta against this regime because they had tortured my father. While that is enough reason to stir my anger against them, the sacrifice of my grandparents and their generation is what keeps me going.

Farida's father also suffered greatly. For opposing the regime he was arrested and tortured on multiple occasions. Farida once described her father's back as looking like the back of a slave because of how many scars he bore from the whippings that he endured. He also suffered broken toes and broken ribs. On one occasion they also attempted to castrate Farida's father with electric cords.

Farida herself has also been a target because of her activism. There have been many death threats made against her by people in the government. Farida became an American citizen in 2016 because the government of Togo denied her of her passport since 2013, which prevented her from being able to travel. During a particularly violent crackdown against protesters in April 2017, soldiers were sent to a farm that is owned by Farida's father to beat and arrest people there in order to send a direct message to her.

As I said, Farida has been involved in the fight against the dictatorship in Togo since she was a teenager. In 2003 her father was arrested along with other activists. Farida was thirteen years old at the time and it was very shocking for her to see how her father was mistreated. The soldiers that arrested him also destroyed everything in their house in an attempt to find evidence against Farida's father. Over time Farida would become more actively involved in the struggle. In 2009 she started a blog which she used to expose the abuses of the government.

In 2014 the opposition party introduced a bill to reinstate the term limits that were established in the 1992 constitution. The ruling party voted against this bill. Farida decided to publish the phone numbers of the politicians who voted against this bill and urged the Togolese people to call these people to ask them why they voted against the bill, which they did, much to the annoyance of these government officials. Farida has been very relentless in her opposition against the dictatorship in Togo. According to Farida, she was trained like a "German shepherd" to hunt down Gnassingbé and she has been hunting him for many years.

I knew that Farida was a Togolese activist who was fighting for democracy in her country, but what I did not realize until I began following her on social media and reading her writings is that Farida is a Pan-Africanist who is fighting for the liberation of Africa and for the liberation of all African people. Farida's main focus has been on the struggle to liberate Togo from dictatorship because she is from Togo, but she has also helped to tackle the issue of slavery in Mauritania and supported struggles against dictatorships in the Gambia, Chad, Gabon, and other countries. Farida's Pan-African vision includes the diaspora as well. I was very surprised and delighted when she told me that her goal was to one day make Togolese citizenship available for all African people in the diaspora so that they can return home if they choose to do so.

Farida let me know that I was one of the few Pan-Africanists who practiced what I preached. She explained to me that when she was living in Washington D.C. she met many people who claimed to be Pan-Africanists, but never actually supported the people of Africa in their struggles for liberation. I knew exactly what she meant because I have my own issues with those who claim to be Pan-Africanists, but never engaged in any sort of real Pan-African organizing or activities. Working to support the struggle in Togo provided me with an opportunity to demonstrate what true Pan-Africanism looks like.

Over the next few months I would continue to remain in communication with Farida regarding the struggle in Togo. This included a two part interview that I conducted with Farida for Huffington Post in December of 2017. The interview was meant to be three parts, but between Farida's busy schedule and Huffington Post ending their contributor platform the third part of the interview was never concluded. I also guest-hosted an interview with Farida on the Steelpan Vibes radio show. I would later also guest-host an interview with Wolali Alijah, who is a member of the Togolese Civil League along with Farida.

Why is the struggle in Togo relevant to Africans in the United States? This is a question that has come up a few times since I have been writing about and speaking about the struggle in Togo. As a Pan-Africanist who believes that the struggles of all African people are interconnected it is very natural for me to support Togo's struggle, but I also recognize that not everyone understands the connection between our struggles so at times it has been necessary for me to demonstrate the interconnected nature of our struggles. This of course is not a new issue. In the 1960s it was necessary for Malcolm X to explain: "I, for one, would like to impress, especially upon those who call themselves leaders, the importance of realizing the direct connection between the struggle of the

Afro-American in this country and the struggle of our people all over the world. As long as we think—as one of my good brothers mentioned out of the side of his mouth here a couple of Sundays ago—that we should get Mississippi straightened out before we worry about the Congo, you'll never get Mississippi straightened out. Not until you start realizing your connection with the Congo."

In the work that I have been doing it has been necessary to get Africans in the United States to understand their connection with Togo. In the first place, many of us can trace our roots to Togo. Togo is located in the region of Africa that was formerly known as the "Slave Coast" because of how many Africans were taken from there. This connection is more than an ancestral connection, however. African people are victimized by an international white supremacist capitalist system which exploits us and enriches itself through that exploitation.

In the particular case of the Africans who live in the United States, we find ourselves impoverished and neglected in the wealthiest nation in the world—a nation whose wealth is built largely through slave labor. Take Orlando, Florida, where I reside, for example. Griffin Park is a federal housing project in Orlando and it is so impoverished and neglected that many of the residents suffer from the effects of air pollution. The decrepit air-conditioning systems have also caused problems for residents as well. This is the type of poverty and neglect that people of African descent live in.

What makes our situation worse is that we are taxpayers. We pay taxes to politicians whom we also elect. These politicians do nothing for us as we struggle in poverty. Our tax money also goes towards paying the same police officers who harass, brutalize, and kill us. We are in effect being made to finance the same political system which oppresses us.

African Americans are also being made to finance the oppression that goes on in Africa, including Togo. As I will explain in the next chapter, the United States has supported the regime in Togo over the years. This support has included developmental aid, as well as military assistance. So American taxes go towards helping to assist a military regime which violently oppresses its own people. The same American system that neglects people of African descent who live in the United States can find the funds to send foreign aid to a dictator.

Just as African Americans are neglected by the American government, the people of Togo have been neglected by the international forces that aid the regime in Togo. This is why my primary work in regards to supporting the struggle in Togo has been to raise awareness and to inform people about the struggle of the Togolese people.

Understanding American foreign policy in Togo and other parts of Africa also has important implications for understanding the question of integration. African Americans must understand that the American system is a system that is built on exploitation and that to become integrated into the system as it exists is to become a part of that system which is built on the exploitation of African people.

It means becoming part of that exploitation.

We can best understand this by looking at the presidency of Barack Obama. In a sense Obama achieved the greatest thing that a black man could hope to achieve in America, which is becoming the president of the country. This achievement was of great symbolic importance to African Americans, yet materially the system had not changed. The Obama administration continued to support the dictators in Africa like Gnassingbé and he also continued America's military expansion in Africa through the Africa Command (AFRICOM), which was initiated by George W. Bush. America's neocolonial policy in Africa continued even after Obama was elected, which is no different from how the colonial system was maintained in place in Africa even as African leaders took over power from their colonial masters.

It is important that as African Americans struggle to free themselves and advance their own interests that they recognize the system which they struggle against is one which oppresses all people of African descent, so we all share a common struggle against common foes. The same system which allows for a police officer to kill a black child in the United States and escape without facing justice is the same system that allows for military forces to kill a black child in Togo and also escape without facing justice. The other thing to keep in mind is that the system is also content to ignore these injustices. In the United States we hardly see much about police brutality or black suffering in the media unless African Americans are out in the streets protesting and marching. Likewise, the little attention that the people of Togo have received from the American media has usually been whenever they are protesting. Otherwise, the people of Togo were expected to suffer in silence just as African Americans are expected to suffer in silence.

This is also connected to the aim of the Movement for Restoring the African Mind. There are those, such as Jesse Lee Peterson, who thanked God for slavery because slavery took his ancestors away from Africa. The Africans like this are Africans whose minds have been corrupted in such a way that they allow themselves to become part of the very system that oppresses their own people. The people who think this way have no regard for the suffering that the American empire has inflicted on African people around the world because they see themselves as being part of that system. This is not only true of African Americans like Peterson who try to distance themselves from their African roots, but also of the African dictators like Faure who oppress their own people for the benefit of their colonial masters. We must develop a new way of thinking which recognizes the global nature of the African struggle and recognizes our connection to Africa. In doing so we will recognize that Togo's struggle is our struggle as well.

2 UNDERSTANDING TOGO'S STRUGGLE

"Psychologically, the domination of the dictator has to be rejected. The population must learn to despise the falsehoods which surround the man; they must refuse to accept that he has any halo of greatness around him. They must remove any confusion in their own minds and see the dictator clearly for what he is—a villain and a monster, the principal enemy of the people."
-Dr. Walter Rodney

"We have been denied of our basic human right. The only right we are allowed to have in Togo is the right to die and today we have chosen to use that right to die for our country if need be."
-Farida Nabourema

Like all African nations, Togo's history within the last few centuries has been a history of constant struggle for liberation against European colonizers and their African allies. Togo was one of the many African nations that were impacted by the slave trade. In fact, Togo was located in the region of West Africa that was known as the Slave Coast because of how many Africans were taken from that region. This region also encompassed present day Benin and Nigeria as well.

Little Popo, which is today known as Aného in Togo, was one of the largest centers of slave trading activity in the Slave Coast. The people of Little Popo were frequently at war with many neighboring kingdoms, including Dahomey. Prisoners of these wars were captured and sold into slavery. The Portuguese were the first set of Europeans to trade for slaves in Little Popo, but slave trading activity in Little Popo would increase significantly when the Dutch and the British became involved. The French and the Danes were also involved in the slave trade in Little Popo as well.

The slave trade had a very destructive impact on African society. The European slave traders instigated conflicts or exploited existing conflicts in Africa, so the areas of Africa which were tangled up in the European slave trade experienced frequent wars and instability. Many parts of Africa were also depopulated due to the slave trade and families were broken up. Olaudah Equiano, who became an abolitionist in Britain, was kidnapped along with his sister and the two were separated before being sold. In his autobiography Equiano described this experience as follows:

When we went to rest the following night they

offered us some victuals; but we refused it; and the only comfort we had was in being in one another's arms all that night, and bathing each other with our tears. But alas! we were soon deprived of even the small comfort of weeping together. The next day proved a day of greater sorrow than I had yet experienced; for my sister and I were then separated, while we lay clasped in each other's arms. It was in vain that we besought them not to part us; she was torn from me, and immediately carried away, while I was left in a state of distraction not to be described. I cried and grieved continually; and for several days I did not eat any thing but what they forced into my mouth.

The abolition of the slave trade was followed by the Scramble for Africa, in which most of Africa was conquered and colonized by the invading European powers. Togoland became a German protectorate in 1884. German rule in Togo was brutal. The Togolese people were often forced to labor for little or no pay. Floggings were one of the means that was used to force the population to labor for the colonialists.

German Togoland was one of the battlegrounds during World War I. On August 26, 1914 the Germans were defeated and were forced to surrender the colony to the British and French forces. Togoland was then partitioned between the British and the French. British Togoland and French Togoland were officially mandated by the League of Nations in 1922. British Togoland would eventually become part of Ghana and French Togoland would go on to become the Togolese Republic.

The splintering of German Togoland between the British and French caused some tensions between Ghana and Togo following independence, but Cameroon was even more severely impacted. Following World War I, German Cameroon was partitioned between the French and the British. The two regions were unified again in 1961 when the British Cameroons voted to become part of Cameroon. Since this unification, those living in the English speaking region have complained about having French being imposed on them and due to years of being neglected and mistreated some in the Anglophone region of Cameroon have been demanding secession from Cameroon.

French rule in Togo was also harsh and exploitative. One incident that illustrates the oppressive nature of French rule occurred in 1932 when the French administration attempted to impose new taxes on the Lomé market women. This sparked widespread protesting from the market women. The protest achieved its aims, but it also demonstrated that unless African people, particularly African women, were protesting in massive numbers then their concerns were of little regard to the colonial governments that ruled over them.

The Togolese people put up fierce resistance against both the German and French colonizers. The Germans fought the Konkomba people in 1897 and 1898 before finally subduing them. The Germans also fought the Kabye in 1900. The Tchokossi (also known as Anoufu) did not come into direct confrontation with the Germans. The Germans had actually entered into an alliance with the Tchokossi to assist in defeating the Konkomba and Kabye. The Tchokossi would fight the French, however. In that conflict the Tchokossi ruler Nabiema Bonsafo was killed. The Konkomba fought the French colonizers as well and lost about 3,000 warriors in that conflict.

Togo became independent from France in 1960 and Sylvanus Olympio became Togo's first president. Olympio was the descendant of Afro-Brazilians who returned to Togo—aside from Togo, Brazilian returnees also settled in Ghana, Nigeria, and Benin. Following independence Olympio had to contend with the fact that during the colonial period Togo was developed in a way that was beneficial for France. Olympio noted:

> The effect of the policy of the colonial powers has been the economic isolation of peoples who live side by side, in some instances within a few miles of each other, while directing the flow of resources to the metropolitan countries. For example, although I can call Paris from my office telephone here in Lomé, I cannot place a call to Lagos in Nigeria only 250 miles away. Again, while it takes a short time to send an air-mail letter to Paris, it takes several days for the same letter to reach Accra, a mere 132 miles away.

Not only was it faster to send a letter to France than Ghana, but there were also tensions between Togo and Ghana because of the colonial borders. These tensions also hindered cooperation between the two nations. Kwame Nkrumah wanted to annex Togo. Olympio opposed this, however. Olympio did not believe that unity between Ghana and Togo meant that one country should be absorbed into the other one. The relationship between the two men was also strained due to several assassination plots against both men, which they each blamed on the other. The situation reached a point where Ghana harbored political dissidents from Togo and Togo did the same for dissidents from Ghana.

Olympio was assassinated in 1963. Prior to his assassination Olympio was planning to remove Togo from the CFA Franc currency and issue Togo its own currency. Shortly after Togo began taking the steps to print its own currency Olympio was assassinated in a French supported coup. Nicolas Grunitzky was placed in power by the military following this coup. Grunitzky was a political rival of Olympio's. Prior to independence, Grunitzky served as the Prime Minister of Togo from 1956 until 1958. Unlike Olympio, Grunitzky did not want complete independence from France. Grunitzky lost to Olympio in the general elections in 1958. In 1967 Gnassingbé Eyadéma, who was one of the leaders in the plot to kill Olympio, overthrew Grunitzky and installed himself as the president of Togo. He would remain in power until his death in 2005 at the age of 69.

Under Eyadéma's rule torture and murder were

commonplace. Amnesty International reported on the specific case of a man named Kouma Sam. A witness to Sam's death explained: "He had his left foot shackled to his right hand and his right foot shackled to his left hand and he was beaten in that position. Then he was tied to the table and the police hit him with cycle lock chain, cables, belts and batons until he lost consciousness. When he came to, he asked for water which was refused. Water was poured over him in revenge. He was vomiting blood which was also coming out of his nostrils. Some detainees put him in a van to go to the infirmary and three days later I learned of his death." Incidents like this in which people are beaten to death are regular occurrences in Togo.

Often times these victims are not even given proper burials. One survivor explained: "I was on my bike when I saw some dead bodies on the roadside. I was questioning passers-by who were around when the military detained me and threw me in a truck. They put me in the middle like a football and assaulted me with kicks, fists and rifle butts. Three people were beaten in the same way as me and they died. Their bodies were left on the roadside." In 1998, during the presidential election campaign, hundreds of people were executed. Among those who were killed included even members of the military. Many of the bodies were later retrieved from the beaches in Togo and Benin. One Beninese fisherman recalled seeing hundreds of bodies floating in the sea.

One of the most well-known examples of the brutality of Eyadéma's regime was the assassination of prominent government critic Tavio Amorin. Amorin, who was a political leader with the Pan-African Socialist Party, returned to Togo in 1991 after living in exile. Amorin was assassinated on July 23, 1992. As he was waiting for a car at the side of the road after visiting a sick relative, two people opened fire on him. He was taken to a hospital in Paris where he died. The assassins left behind identity cards which revealed that the two assassins were police officers. Neither of the assassins was ever brought to justice.

The 1992 constitution established a two term limit for the president, but this was amended in 2002 to allow Eyadéma to run for a third term in 2003. He won that election and died two years later. Under the constitution of Togo the speaker of parliament was to take over as president, but the military moved to install Eyadéma's son, Faure Gnassingbé, as president. International pressure forced Gnassingbé to hold elections. Over 1,000 Togolese citizens were killed during this election. Gnassingbé won that election and won the elections again in 2010 and 2015.

Under Gnassingbé, Togo has been one of the poorest and most miserable countries in Africa. This has been a country where some parts of the population do not have access to clean drinking water. Hospitals are dilapidated and women are even made to give birth on the floor. The prisons in Togo are overpopulated. Not only are prisoners barely fed, but the unsanitary conditions of these prisons have caused some prisoners to become ill and even die from preventable diseases. Poor road conditions have led to many fatal car accidents in Togo. Not only has the regime in Togo killed its citizens through physical violence, but the poor management of Togo has caused hundreds of deaths due to preventable illnesses and preventable accidents.

The protests against the regime that began in August 2017 certainly was not the first time that the people of Togo protested this regime. There were protests in 2010 and 2015 after Gnassingbé was reelected. In 2012 Togolese women called for a sex strike in an attempt to motivate the men of the country to take action. That same year there were protests against the regime which were broken up when the security forces fired teargas at the protesters. There were also protests in February 2017 over fuel price hikes.

This is the background to the protests that began in August 2017. An understanding of Togo's history is necessary for understanding the scope of the struggle being waged there because it is a continuation of centuries of struggle against oppression. The most immediate challenge that the people of Togo face in their struggle is the unrelenting brutality of the regime which they are struggling against. In February 2018 the African Youth Coalition for Democracy and Development, along with the African Network for Human Rights and Solidarity Initiatives released a report which revealed that since the protests began in Togo in August more than 100 people were killed. Among those killed included children. Thousands of others were wounded by bullets or beatings, and some of those victims were handicapped for life. Thousands more were arrested or displaced in the crisis.

This is a regime that has responded to the peaceful protests by opening fire on crowds of people or going house to house to beat and arrest protesters. In one particular incident the police fired teargas into a home and a mother had to rescue her infant who was suffocated by the teargas. This is the type of brutality that the government of Togo is willing to unleash on its own people in order to retain power. The regime is able to carry out such acts of abuse because there are no international forces that have stepped in to pressure the regime to cease its brutality against its own citizens. The situation in Togo is an example of the role that the international community has played in the misrule that continues to plague Africa. The Gnassingbé regime has lasted five decades in power largely through the support of Western countries, as well as failures on the part of intergovernmental institutions in Africa to resolve political issues such as Togo's.

As pointed out earlier, Olympio was assassinated in a French supported coup because he was attempting to make his country truly independent of France. France and other nations that support the regime in Togo do so because that regime serves their interests. Not only do Western governments provide support for the regime in Togo, but there is also the lack of support provided for those who are fighting for democracy in Togo. A report from Amnesty International in 1999, which was titled "Togo: Rule of Terror", noted:

In spite of the gravity of the human rights situation, certain governments, principally European ones, including Germany, Belgium, France and Switzerland, exercise a blanket refusal to applications from Togolese asylum seekers. These governments know full well that some of these asylum seekers are in danger. Although the files of asylum seekers are examined on a case by case basis, the actual human rights situation in Togo is not taken into account and many are returned home. Some of these asylum seekers have been arrested on their arrival in Togo.

The report was especially critical of France's relationship with the Togolese government. The report noted that in 1993, France suspended their aid to Togo after a massacre that took place in January, but resumed cooperation a year later. The brief suspension was also ineffective since assistance that was committed before the suspension was still implemented in spite of the suspension. France not only provided military aid and equipment, but France also assisted with the maintenance and repair of this military equipment as well. Eyadéma's relationship with France was so close that when he died the former president of France, Jacques Chirac, described the dictator as a personal friend. Indeed, France has made it a habit of befriending African dictators.

The dictatorship in Togo has also enjoyed a close relationship with Israel. In October 2017 there was an Israel-Africa summit that was scheduled to take place in Togo, but the event had to be postponed due to the ongoing unrest in Togo. Israel has continued to maintain diplomatic relations with Togo and provides Togo with aid, in spite of the human rights abuses that are carried out by Gnassingbé's government. In return Togo has supported Israel's causes on the international stage. The best example of this was when the United States decided to move its embassy to Jerusalem and recognize Jerusalem as Israel's capital. The United Nations General Assembly rejected this decision. The overwhelming majority of countries voted in favor of a resolution which rejected America's decision. The only African nation to vote in favor of the United States and Israel on this issue was Togo.

Gnassingbé has also enjoyed close ties with the United States. This has included being hosted at the White House where he met President Obama. In 2012, Hillary Clinton, who was serving as the Secretary of State in the Obama administration, visited Togo and met with Gnassingbé. Clinton said: "The United States will be a partner to the government of Togo as it builds on its recent democratic gains, brings dissenting voices to the table for an inclusive dialogue, increases the political participation of women, and carries out a successful constitutional reform process." There were no democratic gains to speak of nor was there a serious attempt to bring dissenting voices to the table. When the people of Togo began protesting in 2017, that same government used violent force to repress and kill those dissenting voices. The response from Hillary Clinton was silence, but when the people of Iran began protests in December of that same year Clinton very publicly expressed her support for the people of Iran.

The government of Togo also won the favor of Donald Trump's administration for being the only African nation to vote against the United Nations' resolution. Much like the previous presidential administrations, the Trump administration has tolerated the regime in Togo because it serves America's interests. This is why, like Hillary Clinton, Trump refused to speak about the protests in Togo, but expressed public support for the protests in Iran.

President Trump's foreign policy in Africa has been the same as previous administrations in that it tolerates dictatorships in Africa so long as those dictators serve American interests. An example of this is Joseph Kabila in the Democratic Republic of Congo. Kabila's term as president was meant to end in 2016, but he postponed the elections. Nikki Haley, the American Ambassador to the United Nations, responded to this by urging Kabila to hold elections in 2018. This was too long for the people of the Congo to wait, so there were protests for Kabila's removal in December 2017. The government responded to the protests by cracking down on the protests with violent force that resulted in several deaths. Despite this and other abuses that have been committed by Kabila's government, the United States took the position of patiently allowing Kabila to wait until the end of 2018 to hold elections.

Since Faure Gnassingbé has been the president of Togo he has received millions of dollars in foreign aid from the United States and there has been no outcry from the American government about the abuses that are carried out in Togo.

The failure of the international community to address the situation in Togo is not only the result of neocolonial policies in which powerful Western nations continue to support African puppets who do their bidding, but it is also a failure on the part of African leaders who have not yet developed effective intergovernmental institutions that address internal African issues. One of those existing institutions that have failed the people of Togo is the Economic Community of West African States (ECOWAS) of which Togo is a member state. On June 4, 2017, Faure Gnassingbé was selected as the chairperson for ECOWAS. He continued to remain in this capacity even as his government violently repressed the protesters and there was no pressure placed on Gnassingbé to cease his brutalities or to relinquish his position.

ECOWAS has never been committed to ensuring that member states uphold democracy and human rights. The first chairperson of ECOWAS was Yakubu Gowon, who came to power in a military coup in Nigeria. Gnassingbé Eyadéma served as the chairperson in 1975. Eyadéma was followed by Olusegun Obasanjo, who led a violently repressive military regime in Nigeria. Mathieu Kérékou, who came to power in Benin as the result of a military coup, served as the chairperson from 1982 until 1983. Lansana Conté of Guinea served as the chairperson from 1984 until 1985. He too came to power in a military coup and oversaw a repressive military regime that engaged in human rights abuses. Thomas Sankara was denied the ability to serve as the chairman of ECOWAS, but Blaise Compaoré, the man responsible for the coup that killed Sankara, served as the chairman of ECOWAS.

When the military first installed Faure Gnassingbé as the president of Togo, ECOWAS imposed sanctions on Togo and refused to recognize the new regime. The pressure did force Gnassingbé to step down and hold elections. Those elections ended with more than one thousand Togolese citizens being killed. Despite the electoral violence and the charges of electoral fraud, ECOWAS lifted the sanctions and recognized Gnassingbé as the president of Togo. As the human rights abuses continued and more fraudulent elections were held in Togo, ECOWAS refused to put any sort of pressure on the regime in Togo for the purpose of producing democratic changes.

What has been especially disappointing about ECOWAS' lack of urgency in handling the situation in Togo is the fact that ECOWAS has demonstrated that it can move quickly to deal with situations like this. Following the 2016 presidential election in the Gambia the opposition leader Adama Barrow defeated Yahya Jammeh. Jammeh refused to step down from power, however. In January 2017, ECOWAS decided to send military forces into the Gambia which forced Jammeh to concede defeat. At the very least ECOWAS could mobilize troops in

Togo to ensure that protesters are able to protest peacefully without being brutalized by the government, but the difference between Togo and the Gambia is that ECOWAS recognizes Gnassingbé as the elected president of Togo, despite the fraudulent elections that are held in Togo. Those fraudulent elections allow Gnassingbé to maintain the façade of being a democratically elected president, whereas Jammeh was very blatantly undermining the democratic institutions of his country by refusing to accept the election results. Yet another advantage that Gnassingbé has over Jammeh is that Gnassingbé was serving as the chairperson of ECOWAS when the protests against him began. What is more is that Marcel Alain de Souza, who was the acting ECOWAS Commission President at the time that the protests in Togo began, is married to Gnassingbé's sister.

Apart from these international forces which the people of Togo must overcome in order to free themselves from dictatorial rule, there is also the issue of national institutions which must be developed as well. For the five decades that the Gnassingbé regime has been in power the most dominant governmental institution has been that of the military. Togo achieved its independence on April 27, 1960 under the leadership of Sylvanus Olympio and his political party, the Committee for the Unity of Togo (CUT). One of the challenges that Olympio was forced to confront was the military. Gnassingbé Eyadéma served as a soldier in the colonial French army. During the Algerian War, Eyadéma fought on the side of the French colonizers who were trying to retain their domination of Algeria. When Togo became independent from France many former colonial soldiers like Eyadéma found themselves without a job. They were no longer soldiers in the colonial French army nor were they included as members of the newly formed army of Togo.

Part of Olympio's attempt to break away from the French colonial influence was to develop a national army that did not include those who were soldiers for the former colonial power. It was some of the same people that Olympio excluded from Togo's army that would ultimately assassinate him. As a soldier in the colonial army Eyadéma served the interests of France and he continued to do so once he became the president of Togo. Eyadéma was able to establish close ties with the former colonial power and he dutifully served their interests, but this has not always been the case for former soldiers of the colonial empires who came into power. France intervened in the Central African Republic by overthrowing David Dacko and installing Jean-Bedel Bokassa, who served in the French army during World War II and the Indo-China war. France supported Bokassa, but the brutalities of his regime became too much for even them to ignore and they sent troops into the Central African Republic to topple Bokassa and put Dacko back in power.

Idi Amin was recruited to serve in the King's African Rifles in Kenya. Amin was barely literate, but he was someone with a large physique and great athletic ability. He was the national heavyweight boxing champion for several years. He was able to win the favor of British officers due to his loyalty and the role he played in helping to brutally suppress the Mau Mau rebellion in Kenya. Amin eventually rose to the rank of sergeant major, which was the highest position available to an African in the colonial army. Amin became the president of Uganda in 1971 after a coup which overthrew Milton Obote. The British opted to recognize Amin's government and provided support for him, but the relationship between Amin and Britain became strained over time due to Amin's uncontrollable and unpredictable behavior.

The military regimes that emerged in Africa following independence are a direct product of colonialism's legacy in Africa. Under colonialism it was necessary to establish security forces for the purpose of controlling the colonized population. After gaining independence, many African nations continued to use these security forces for the purpose of maintaining domination over the African masses. The military regimes are an example of how colonialism uprooted African traditions and replaced them with repressive institutions.

Armies in pre-colonial African societies operated very differently. This is a point that George Ayittey made in "Democracy and Africa", where he writes:

> It is also true that many African societies were made up of warriors. But military rule was not part of indigenous African culture. In indigenous African societies, the people were the army, owning their own weapons. In the

event of imminent war, the chief would summon all young men of a certain age-grade to assemble and then lead them into battle. After cessation of hostilities, the "army" was disbanded and the "soldiers" or warriors went about their normal activities. In most places, there was no military involvement in the indigenous system of government.

Ayittey points out that a small number of African societies had standing armies. This included Asante, Dahomey, Yoruba, and the Zulus. He also notes that in those societies the "armies cultivated their own farms to feed themselves, built and maintained roads, protected their citizens, scarcely acting as a drain on the native economies." The national armies that were formed after independence took on a much different role. They were often used to repress the masses in order to keep corrupt regimes in power. In some cases, such as Togo, the army was not only an institution used by a dictator to retain power, but the army itself seized power and controlled the country.

In many African countries the military and security forces are among some of the strongest institutions of the state because they are necessary to buttress the often incompetent and corrupt governments. Due to the weak political institutions and the strength of the military, often times the army steps in and takes control of the country. In Dahomey, for example, the army overthrew President Hubert Maga in 1963 following unrest in the country. Maga's corruption and misrule caused a crisis in the country, so the army stepped in to resolve the issue. In Burundi, Michel Micombero helped to put down a coup attempt against Mwambutsa IV. Micombero would later help to organize a coup to put Ntare V in power before Micombero decided to lead a coup of his own which abolished the monarchy in Burundi and established military rule. The same army that helped to maintain the monarchy in Burundi eventually overthrew the monarchy altogether.

Another example of the military taking over the role of governing was in Chad. François Tombalbaye became the first president of Chad when the country obtained its independence from France in 1960. Tombalbaye's government quickly became an autocratic one. Gabriel Lisette, a colonial administrator who was born in Panama and posted to Chad in 1946, founded the Chadian Progressive Party (PPT). Tombalbaye, a former teacher who became a brick-maker, eventually took over leadership of the PPT. One week before Chad became independent Tombalbaye purged Lisette from the PPT and declared him a noncitizen of Chad. Lisette was of African descent, but he was born in Panama and this was used as a justification for him being purged from the ruling party. Lisette was traveling abroad when this announcement was made and he was barred from returning to Chad. This was the first example of the extremes that Tombalbaye would go to in order to eliminate potential political opponents.

In January 1962, Tombalbaye banned all political parties but the PPT and began arresting political opponents. Tombalbaye's government was particularly repressive toward Muslims, which resulted in some of the Muslims in Chad rebelling against the government by attacking and killing government officials. Making matters worse was the government's ineffective response to a drought that was taking place. Tombalbaye was quickly losing popularity among every segment of society in Chad, including the army and on April 13, 1975, members of the army decided to assassinate Tombalbaye and established a military government.

The coup that brought Thomas Sankara into power in Burkina Faso was an exception in African politics in that the military government that Sankara headed actually made significant advancements in Burkina Faso. Sankara did not establish a military regime in which those in the government used their position to enrich themselves at the expense of the masses. This was the exception, but the norm has been that military coups have led to very corrupt and violently repressive regimes.

One of the issues with military rule is that often once the military seizes power it then creates a precedent for which violence and force can be used for the transference of power. It creates a cycle of violence and instability. Some of the African nations that have been mentioned previously serve as examples of this. In the Central African Republic, David Dacko returned to power again in 1979 only to be deposed again in 1981 by André Kolingba, who remained in power until 1993 when Ange-Félix Patassé was elected as the president of the Central African Republic. The Central African

Republic was independent since 1960 and it was not until 1993 that the country would see its first peaceful transfer of power. The coups would continue, however. In 2003, François Bozizé seized power through a coup. He remained in power until 2013 when he was forced into exile when rebels seized power.

In Uganda, Milton Obote eventually came back into power after Idi Amin was deposed. Obote was deposed yet again in 1985. This led to a civil war in Uganda which resulted in Yoweri Museveni becoming president in 1986. Thousands of Ugandans were killed in the war and among the human rights violations that were committed during this war included the use of child soldiers. Rebellion and war continued in Uganda after Museveni became president. The rebel groups that have fought Museveni's government include the Holy Spirit Movement which was led by Alice Auma and Joseph Kony's Lord's Resistance Army.

Niger became independent of France in 1960. By 1974 Hamani Diori, Niger's first president, was overthrown in a military coup. The people of Niger grew weary of Diori's corruption and misrule, so the military decided to stage a coup and take power. Since then Niger has experienced several coups. The most recent came in 2010 when President Mamadou Tandja attempted to extend his mandate after his term had ended. The military stepped in and overthrew Tandja.

These examples are also relevant for understanding the resolution to Togo's crisis, as well as the crisis faced by other African nations that are ruled by dictators. The people of Togo have decided to protest the regime in Togo through non-violent civil disobedience. On some occasions protesters have resorted to defending themselves from aggression by fighting back, but by and large the revolt that is taking place in Togo is not a violent revolt. This is important because we have seen in Africa, time and time again, that violent seizures of power have led to cycles of violence and conflicts that have taken decades to resolve. For this reason it is preferable that the crisis in Togo be resolved through a peaceful transfer of power, rather than through a violent seizure of power.

Of course, given the structure of the regime in Togo a military coup there would be unlikely. In Zimbabwe the military stepped in and ousted Robert Mugabe in 2017 after Mugabe had purged members of the government, including Vice President Emmerson Mnangagwa. The military decided to step in to end the purges by ousting Mugabe, in yet another example of the military in Africa being used to resolve political issues. In this case Mugabe fell out of favor with certain segments of the armed forces, but this is unlikely to happen in Togo where the Gnassingbé regime has built up a military that is completely loyal to the dictator. The majority of the military is made up of Eyadéma's ethnic group, the Kabye. Aside from fostering a military that is built on tribal loyalties, the Togolese military is also made up of people who are incompetent. Their only qualifications for being in the positions that they are in is their undying loyalty to the regime. Some of the members of the military are barely literate, yet they hold very influential positions in the military. For example, Felix Abalo Kadanga, who was appointed as the chief of the Togolese army in 2013, infamously misspelled the word *paix*, which is the French word for peace.

Apart from the military seizing power, there have also been cases in which civilians have taken up arms against corrupt regimes. This has been problematic as well. In many cases rebels in Africa, who may have legitimate grievances against the governments which they fight end up committing atrocities of their own. Rebel groups throughout Africa have engaged in murdering, mutilating, torturing, and raping civilians. We have seen examples of this on the part of rebels in countries such as Nigeria, Uganda, the Central African Republic, Sierra Leone, Liberia, Sudan, the Democratic Republic of Congo, and Rwanda, to name a few countries. In Togo's situation there are segments of the population that have become so frustrated and fed up with the brutalities that they have been openly considering arming themselves for a violent rebellion, but this will be difficult because those who oppose the government do not even possess the resources and training required for any type of sustained armed rebellion. If the situation in Togo does reach a point where the protesters organize armed rebel groups it will have been because the government has driven the Togolese people to such extremes. It will also have been because the international community would have failed to help bring about a peaceful resolution to the crisis in Togo.

Elections in Togo are fraudulent, so voting Gnassingbé out of power has never been an option for the people of Togo. Aside from voting Gnassingbé out of power or overthrowing the government through a violent revolution, the only option available to the people of Togo to create regime change is through civil disobedience, which is what they have been attempting to do. The people of Togo are effectively refusing to be governed by the regime with the intent of eventually forcing the dictator to give in to their demands.

This was a strategy that worked for the people of Haiti. Like Togo, Haiti endured decades of being ruled by a father-son dictatorship. When François Duvalier died his son Jean-Claude Duvalier took over and continued his father's brutal regime. The Duvalier dynasty finally came to an end in 1986 when the people of Haiti rose up in protest. The protests began in 1984 and continued until 1986. The protests eventually forced Duvalier to flee the country. This is what the people of Togo are hoping to achieve as well.

For the people of Togo defeating the dictator is just the first step. Haiti was mentioned as an example where the masses were able to topple a repressive dictatorial regime that was passed down from father to son, but the end of dictatorship in Haiti has not meant the end to corruption and mismanagement in the government. This has also been the case in African countries which were formerly under the control of dictatorships. The end of dictatorship in those countries was not an end to incompetence and corruption within the government.

The dictatorship has to be replaced by a truly democratic system. This does not mean democracy simply in the sense of having fair and free elections, but democracy in that the political system that replaces the existing one in Togo must be transparent and allow for the freedom of expression on the part of citizens. This also means a system which places checks on those who are in power. In Antigua, for example, Vere Bird was democratically elected as the prime minister. He did not come to power in a military coup, yet many similar features of nepotism and corruption existed in Antigua. I mention Vere Bird specifically because the Bird family essentially controlled Antigua during the period that he was prime minister and after Vere Bird resigned his son Lester Bird took over as the prime minister of the country. After a scandal in which Israeli produced guns were smuggled from Antigua to a drug cartel in Colombia, angry protesters in Antigua carried signs that declared "The Birds Must Go!" The people of Antigua not only wanted Vere Bird out of power, but they wanted the entire Bird family out of politics in Antigua because that family was using its political position to enrich itself at the expense of the people of Antigua, just as the Gnassingbé family has done in Togo.

Antigua never became the outright dictatorial state that Togo and Haiti became, yet the same features of one family rule existed in Antigua. Elections alone do not guarantee democratic representation nor do they prevent the abuse of power, so democracy in Togo has to mean more than having fair and free elections. This will be one of the challenges that Togo faces once Gnassingbé is removed from power. African countries that have already put an end to outright dictatorship are already dealing with these issues. For example, Adama Barrow was democratically elected in the Gambia and despite taking over power from a brutal dictatorship Barrow's government has demonstrated authoritarian tendencies such as when the Gambian police arrested and questioned a university lecturer named Ismaila Ceesay for comments that he made regarding the president. Nigeria is no longer ruled by a military dictatorship, yet the abuse of Nigerian civilians by the Nigerian military continues. The oppressive institutions that sustain a dictator can remain in place even after the dictator is removed.

Developing truly democratic institutions in Togo will be a challenge given that Togo has been ruled by a dictatorship for five decades so there are generations of Togolese people who have never known anything but dictatorial rule. As the example of the Gambia shows, authoritarian practices do not simply disappear once the dictator is removed and democratic elections are put in place, so the end of the dictatorship in Togo will be the beginning of the process of reconstructing Togolese society, but that reconstruction cannot begin until the dictatorship is removed.

The struggle being waged in Togo is also part of a larger struggle against neocolonialism and dictatorial rule across Africa. Togo is of great importance to this struggle because the regime there is the oldest military regime in Africa. A successful revolution in Togo would send the message that no dictatorship in Africa is invincible where the African masses are concerned. This step is especially important because dictators not only use force to maintain their power, but they also use propaganda to foster a cult of personality in order to both satisfy their inflated egos and to present an all-powerful image of themselves to their people. Some of these dictators have become so delusional that they lose touch with reality and begin to believe their own propaganda.

Eyadéma and his son are typical examples of African dictators that have lost touch with reality. Eyadéma went so far as to commission a heroic comic book about his life titled *Il Était Une Fois...Eyadema* (*Once Upon a Time...Eyadema*) because he fancied himself as a superhero. This superhero also built statues of himself and even had his face ingrained on wristwatches. Eyadéma heaped praises unto himself as his people wallowed in poverty and neglect. Faure was so out of touch with reality that the poor man did not even realize he was a dictator! Faure complained that his enemies had used technology to turn a "simple man" such as himself into a "bloody dictator." The only way to cure dictators of their delusions and bring them back to reality is to strip them of their power. As the people of Togo have been demanding, "Faure Must Go!" He must go in order for the people of Togo to be free.

3 AN INTERVIEW WITH FARIDA NABOUREMA

This is a two part interview that I conducted with Farida Nabourema via email in December 2017 for Huffington Post.

Part 1

DWAYNE: How and why did you first become involved in the fight against the dictatorship in Togo?

FARIDA: I got involved as a teenager following the arrestation of my father in 2003 along with some of his comrades and with time I evolved with the struggle.

DWAYNE: Right now the immediate struggle of the Togolese people is to remove Faure Gnassingbe and to restore the 1992 constitution which imposed presidential term limits. One problem that we have seen in many African countries is that the transition from dictatorship to democracy has not eliminated corruption and misrule by the government. Burkina Faso is a very recent example of how removing a dictator does not necessarily mean removing bad governance. Are the activists and political opposition in Togo currently preparing for the challenges that will take place once Faure is removed or will this be an issue that you intend to address after you achieve your immediate objectives?

FARIDA: I honestly believe it is naive to think that the fall of an autocratic government will automatically wipe out bad governance and fix all the issues the society is facing. It took time for all societies to reinvent themselves and establish systems of checks and balances that prevent autocracy on one side and implement mechanisms that reduce corruption on the other side. I know for sure that the post-Gnassingbé Togo will be difficult because all that over 75% of the Togolese people have known is dictatorship. We the people still have a long way to acknowledge the power we have, understand our rights, and most importantly, our responsibilities and duties as citizens. And we might even never get it. Our generation might be a transitional one that will lead other generations into true democracy, but to get there we need to constantly fight for the betterment of our country. Democracy is not an end in itself. It is supposed to be a tool for an equal and fair society in which people can fulfill themselves. So, I think we need to be patient with countries like Burkina Faso who I believe are learning from their mistakes and working hard to rebuild their country that dictatorship held hostage for almost three decades. In Togo we are trying to learn lessons from others' experiences and are anticipating on some of the challenges we will be faced with. But I am not a prophet and cannot predict what it is going to look like. But as an activist, I know anything will be better than being ruled by a family that maintains us in extreme poverty on top of abusing us at every given opportunity when we dare complain about our suffering.

DWAYNE: Something that you have mentioned often about Togo is the role that women have played in the current revolution there. Could you please elaborate on some of the ways that women have played a critical role in Togo's struggle?

FARIDA: Togolese women's involvement in the struggle of the liberation of Togo dates back to the colonial era. Women had less reasons to hold on to colonialism than men as they were completely excluded from the job market, education and politics; probably because these colonial powers operated themselves in very patriarchal systems which transcended onto their colonies. From the struggle for independence to that against dictatorship, Togolese women have been the major sponsors. Unlike men who see commerce and trade as female professions, Togolese women operate in nontraditional sectors and have a reputation of being fierce businesswomen. They invest a lot of money in sponsoring opposition parties which is the reason the government of Faure Gnassingbe burnt down the two largest markets of Togo to not only punish them but to cut the opposition from their main source of income: women. Togolese women's participation is not only financial but also physical and to some extent spiritual. Togo is one of the very few African countries whose vast majority of people resisted religious colonialism by holding onto their traditional beliefs. 51% of Togolese people practice their traditional religion where women play a central role as priestesses, healers and decision makers. These women have organized protests, sex strikes, and all sorts of activities that they believe can spiritually weaken the dictatorship and end the suffering of their children. Although women are not much represented in political offices basically because running for political offices is associated with having a modern education and for a long time women were disadvantaged as the very first schools during western colonialism, both under the Germans and later under the French, excluded women from school. But this is changing as I see more and more women like myself being in the frontline of the struggle and gender has never truly been a handicap for us Togolese women when it comes to participating in politics.

DWAYNE: Not only is imprisonment one of the ways in which the opposition has been suppressed in Togo, but Togo is particularly notorious for its terrible prison conditions. You are probably well-aware that prisons are something that did not exist in Africa prior to colonization. Myself, and others, have also argued that military dictatorships like the one in Togo are also a part of the legacy of colonialism. My question is do you believe that Togo can draw inspiration from pre-colonial institutions and customs to build a better society?

FARIDA: Of course. About 80% of the prison facilities in Togo were built under colonial rule. My father, for example, who has been a political prisoner for several times told me stories of prison guards who told them they learnt their torture practices from the French and the tradition of torture and abuse in prison was sustained by dictatorship. Therefore I strongly believe that we can reduce if not wipe out prisons in Togo, at least as they are used and managed today, by going back to our precolonial society in which crime is defined and handled differently with a stronger focus on restorative justice instead of the retributive one.

DWAYNE: Tribalism has been a problem in many African countries. This obviously has its roots in colonialism's practice of divide and rule, as well as the borders that the Europeans created. Since independence many African leaders have continued to exploit so-called tribal differences for their own benefit. Has tribalism been a serious issue in Togo and do you believe that linguistic, cultural, and religious differences are an obstacle to national unity in Togo?

FARIDA: I will shock you if I tell you that tribalism has never been an issue in Togo. Togo has a very peculiar story. It is a land of refuge of several tribes who fled persecution from all over the places in West Africa. Prior to the establishment of the Germans, most tribes in Togo were not organized under strong monarchies or empires except two in the north. Unlike other countries like Benin and Ghana where you have strong empires like Dahomey and the Ashanti just to name these few, Togo was inhabited basically by refugees who couldn't fight and who live off small scale farming and fishery. So you have there a group of people who themselves fled persecution from other regions and although we have 40 tribes in Togo, there has not been any major tribal crisis that shook the country. Eyadema Gnassingbe, however, with the help of the French tried to sell the myth that his regime was supported by northerners as his own ethnic group is located in the northeastern part of Togo. The reality however is that northern Togo is more ethnically diverse than the south. The Ewe by themselves make up about 40% of the population of Togo and 60% of the population in southern Togo. There are twice more ethnic groups in northern Togo than there are in southern Togo and no ethnic group, including Eyadema's, dominates the north. Both my parents come from two different northern ethnic groups that have both been opposed to the military regime just like the vast majority of other ethnic groups in the country.

Secondly, as I said earlier and I am proud to repeat it, Togo is one of the few African countries that resisted religious colonialism. We have the highest percentage of "animists" as we are referred to on the continent and our ancestral religions are not proselytist therefore sparing us these irrelevant religious fights and competition. Christians and Muslims who represent altogether less than 50% of the population are minorities in each of their ethnic groups and the most amazing thing is that you find them in every ethnic group. This has really helped us avoid religious clashes.

DWAYNE: You have criticized the Economic Community of West African States (ECOWAS) and the African Union (AU) over their handling of the situation in Togo. Do you think these bodies are effective? And if not what do you think would be a better alternative? Kwame Nkrumah envisioned the United States of Africa. Do you think a continental government like the one Nkrumah envisioned would be more effective than the African Union is now?

FARIDA: The inefficacy of the ECOWAS and the AU is done on purpose. Our heads of state have no interest whatsoever in uniting the continent because the vast majority of them do not want to follow rule of law and want to maintain themselves in power through dictatorship. The African Union for example drives about 80% of its funding from the European Union, the United States and China. Their headquarters was donated to them by the Chinese government because our heads of states after 50 years of independence have refused to raise the money required to build it. It is not that we cannot afford to fund our own union but our leaders deliberately refuse to provide both financial and political power to these institutions because reinforcing them translates to weakening their own governments and relinquishing their authoritarian power.

So we the new generation of Africans must fight to get rid of such selfish leaders and work towards the unity of the continent which is the only way we can assure our development. As about Nkrumah's vision for a continental government, it cannot survive the type of leadership and citizenry we currently have. Unfortunately, the current generation of Africans have mostly only known totalitarianism and they are unaware of their duties, rights and responsibilities as citizens. And the current leadership is chronically corrupt. If these guys cannot rule a country at the micro level, it will be a crime to entrust them with a bigger portfolio. Political pan Africanism is an idea we must prepare both African citizens and leaders for. It has to be understood, demanded and implemented by the people. Forcing it on them will be disastrous because the people will resist it.

DWAYNE: What are your personal feelings about Sylvanus Olympio and how much does his vision for Togo influence your work?

FARIDA: I will shock you if I tell you that I know very little about his vision except that he wanted a Togo free from colonialism and he was working not only for the political liberation of Togo but for the economic freedom of my country. Yes he was a brilliant guy but there were other brilliant freedom fighters in Togo and Sylvanus Olympio only got to rule Togo for three years. Eyadema made sure that little is taught about him in schools so there is very little literature available about the guy and I had already developed political consciousness and was already an activist before reading about Olympio through the works of the prominent Togolese historian Godwin Tete who worked with Olympio for so many years and who actually has inspired me more himself than Olympio. The very first African president that has inspired me is Sekou Toure and the second, who is not African but Black, is the Haitian Liberator Toussaint Louverture. I later read about Amilcar Cabral and Patrice Lumumba before reading about Thomas Sankara and Nkrumah after leaving Togo when I was already in college. Later in my college years I was able to expand my knowledge about African and Black Liberators and realized how little we are told about them because our colonial educational programs have not been edited since we got our independence and we are still trained to serve the colonial rule, not to serve our own interests.

Part 2

DWAYNE: The years that Kwame Nkrumah spent

studying in the United States were very influential for him. Not only did he experience American racism, but he also came into contact with many activists and scholars in the United States. It was during his time in the United States that Nkrumah was first introduced to the ideas of Marcus Garvey, which greatly influenced Nkrumah's vision for a united Africa. Like Nkrumah, many political leaders and activists from Africa were influenced by their experiences living in America and Europe. In what ways has living in the United States influenced your activism? Did you experience any racism while you were living in America?

FARIDA: I do not recall experiencing racism directly as an individual when I was living in the United States but my political consciousness allowed me to go beyond myself and identify racist structures that exist within the American society which make it harder for Black people to succeed and live than for many other races. I read a lot more about segregation as a teenager in Togo than I did while living in the United States. So I already came with my own prejudices about the United States and honestly I expected things to be worse for me as a Black girl than it ended up being. I went school at American University which only had 9% of Black students back then and it felt very funny in the beginning but the school is known for being on the liberal side so things weren't bad at all. I might surprise you if I say that living in America enforced my struggle for democracy in Togo for two reasons. One: I so didn't like living in the states that I told myself I must do everything possible to end dictatorship in Togo because I want to go home. And two: I have always felt like we Africans who have voluntarily migrated to the United States were able to do so because those who were forced to settle there as slaves fought for their liberation to ensure that we too can make the United States our home if we so wish. It was African Americans who fought hard for Africans to be included into the Diversity Immigrant Visa Program which is how the majority of Africans were able to migrate to the US during the past two decades. I felt and still feel like we need to reciprocate by fixing Africa and welcoming them home someday. Those of us who got a chance to benefit from the "American Dream" to some extent need to make Africa safe and habitable to all African descents who stood for us even when they didn't have to.

DWAYNE: Aside from the struggle in Togo, what other causes have you been involved in?

FARIDA: I have fought the "Francafrique" system and still am fighting it. African countries that were colonized by the French have never truly been decolonized. We are still using a currency that was imposed on us by the French for which we are keeping 80% of our reserves in the French National Reserve for their own use. We are still paying colonial taxes and have signed a colonial pact with France which gives the French a priority over our market. This system has allowed France to withstand itself as a world power by milking our natural resources, heavily indebting us and, to sustain such injustice, the French give 100% support to the dictators who they either put in power or are helping maintain in power provided they give them what they want. I know that fighting the Gnassingbé regime is only a layer of our struggle because they were put and are kept in power by the French government. Many activists like myself were killed for making statements like this and people remind me of the danger that comes with standing against French neocolonialism but we can't keep staring at the plague and call it a flu.

DWAYNE: Who are some of your greatest influences as an activist?

FARIDA: My father. He raised me as a warrior and he made me one. Then I have Toussaint Louverture. His courage inspires me tremendously and I dream to make Togo a safe haven for all Africans and Black descents as Louverture and Dessalines did with Haiti. Then I have lot of admiration for Sekou Touré for defying the French colonialists and choosing independence over subjugation. I quote him: "we prefer freedom in poverty to wealth in slavery" and that describes who I am and what I am about. I will rather be poor, and free, than allow my subjugation because freedom, at the end of the day, is the greatest wealth. Thomas Sankara is also a great inspiration and influence. He demonstrated that poverty is manmade and was able to accomplish in Burkina Faso, within four years, what no other African head of state was ever able to accomplish within their tenure.

DWAYNE: What motivated you to become a writer?

FARIDA: My father again. I started writing since I was a child. I use to be bullied as a kid and I would get so angry that it made me sick. So my father suggested that I write every time I am angry as a therapeutic solution. I followed his advice and for so many years I only wrote when I am angry and when I started blogging people felt that rage in my writings. Amazingly, most liked it and that's how I started gaining followers because people were connected to my writings, related to my anger over the oppression we put up with and many will come to me to share their stories and ask me to write about it.

DWAYNE: Aside from *La Pression de l'Oppression* have you published any other books? Do you plan to publish any more books in the future?

FARIDA: I have not published any other book yet but I have one that is ready for publication. I am just waiting to do it at the right time when I can genuinely focus on its promotion.

DWAYNE: You are critical of Robert Mugabe and you are also aware that your position on Mugabe is a controversial one because many people support Mugabe. I myself have gotten into serious discussions with both Africans and African Americans over Mugabe. I know many people supported his pro-African and anti-imperialistic rhetoric, while downplaying or ignoring some of his actual policies which have been very harmful for the people of Zimbabwe. How often do you run into this problem of people praising certain leaders for their rhetoric, while also ignoring their policies and actions?

FARIDA: I run into it quite often and I understand where they are coming from. Our struggle has multiple layers but at the end of the day, deep down, we are not fighting for democracy. We are fighting for the freedom of our people from all form of oppression and democracy is a tool to reach that freedom. Some people stop at the first layer: fighting foreign/colonial powers. I see myself there but I also see myself fighting beyond the colonial powers. We've had anti-colonialism leaders in Africa like Sedar Senghor from Senegal who abused their people even more when they rose to power. These people didn't come in because they believed in equality and social justice but because they felt entitled and believed it should be them profiting from the abuse of their people. In Togo, for example, there were former slaves who returned from Brazil who established themselves along the West African coast only to become slave traders themselves. They didn't come as former slaves to liberate their people from colonialism but to enrich themselves and profit from the abusive system. I am not saying that Mugabe is that kind of leader and I have a lot of respect and consideration for some of his achievements in Zimbabwe. But the problem with Mugabe is that he has refused to acknowledge his limitations and not only wanted to maintain himself in power for life, but also comported himself at some point as a king. At some point he felt so entitled and was no longer serving the interest of the people. Any leader who believes there cannot be a better leader than himself is not a good leader. Leaders should strive to prepare stronger successors.

DWAYNE: You have said before that the problem in Africa is not the leadership, but the citizenry. I think African people have been so mentally colonized that very often we passively accept things that we should not accept. I recently launched a movement called the Movement for Restoring the African Mind. This movement seeks to address the wrongheaded thinking that so many of us have. Is this something that you have had to address in your own activism?

FARIDA: I think it is wrong to try to address to the wrongheadedness of people as you put it. It rarely works. It is an impossible mission to try to undo the mindset of adults who were born and raised in a system that trained them to be submissive. You will waste time, energy and effort and be lucky if you survive. What you need to focus on is the young people. Millions are born every year and millions become teenagers and new adults every year. I founded the Faure Must Go movement in 2011 when I was 20 years old. I didn't waste my time talking to older folks who were convinced that nothing can move this regime. I was talking to the younger ones either; as young as myself or much younger. The kids that were 13, 15, 18 in 2011 are the young adults that are driving this revolution today and the elders tag along because they do not want to be left out. I always say that if I was able to become an activist at age 13 then children should not be excluded from politics. It prepares them to be resilient adults who know what they want and go for it. And at that age we are naturally curious so we welcome knowledge and process information faster. Do not try to fix the minds that are already corrupt. Tap into the fresh ones that have not yet been deformed. By 2050 Africa will have the youngest population in the world and right now we already have 60% that are under age 30. We need to be prepared to work with children as they come and put them on the right track.

DWAYNE: When I saw you criticizing Yemi Alade for singing the praises of the dictatorship in Togo it reminded me of the behaviors of some of our artists in the diaspora. I have been very critical of the role that some musicians have played in helping to maintain the oppression of African people here in the diaspora. In the Caribbean there have been situations in which artists have been rewarded by political parties for singing the praises of those parties, no matter how corrupt the political parties that they support may be. And in the United States artists typically are less political in the content of their music, but often times their music promotes very negative or stereotypical images that degrade African Americans and promote the type of wrongheaded mentalities that I mentioned. So for us in the diaspora the musicians have become a serious part of the problem because they promote the type of things that we are fighting against. Based on what you have observed do you see the same problem in Africa in which certain artists play a role in helping to support the institutions and people that oppress Africans?

FARIDA: Artists and athletes have helped promote tyrants in the past and this phenomenon continues. They are what my father will call "nutritional artists" which means they do it for their belly, for the money. Luckily in Togo, and I believe it is the same everywhere else, people did not buy into such propaganda and most of the time it backfired on the artists. However, we have also had artists that contributed to the liberation of their people through their arts. Just a month ago a convoy of musicians were attacked by militaries in Togo and one of them was shot. So we've had artists on both sides. Those who share the pain of their communities and work for its betterment even if it means putting their career or life on the line and those who are into it just for the money.

DWAYNE: What would you say is your greatest achievement as an activist so far?

FARIDA: Faure Must Go. When I said Faure Must

Go almost 8 years ago, people called me all sort of names in Togo. Many thought I was crazy or foolish but I did not give up. I faced the attacks, fought them, kept preaching and today it became the slogan of the struggle. Even those who cannot spell it say it. I burst into laughter when I read a sign: "Faure Must Go". Togo is a French speaking country and most people cannot read or write English. But I chose Faure Must Go not the French version Faure Doit Partir which I could have done. I chose Faure Must Go because the French are going with him and I am proud that I have defied the system at all levels. Faure Must Go would have died if I quit and it cost me so much more than I will ever be willing to reveal for the sake of my family. But today I am very proud that millions of people, the vast majority of my people can say it, write it, chant it, and wear it without fear of retribution.

www.ingramcontent.com/pod-product-compliance
Lightning Source LLC
Chambersburg PA
CBHW070035260726
48658CB00002B/638